INTERMITTENT FAST
OVER 50 CO(

The Complete Collection to Improve Your Health and Detox Your Body While Losing Weight and Boosting Metabolism

BY

MARSH COOK

TABLE OF CONTENTS

INTRODUCTION

Intermittent Fasting, likewise referred to as recurring energy restriction, is an umbrella term for different dish timing routines that cycle in between voluntary Fasting (or decreased calorie consumption) and nonfasting over a given period. Three approaches of intermittent Fasting are alternate-day Fasting, periodic Fasting, and also daily time-restricted feeding. Intermittent Fasting is similar to a calorie-restriction diet. Although being examined in the 21st century as a technique to possibly lower the danger of diet-related illness, recurring Fasting is also regarded as a trend. The science concerning recurring Fasting is opposed. The American Heart Association (AHA) states that intermittent Fasting may generate fat burning, minimize insulin resistance, and reduced the danger of cardiometabolic conditions, although its lasting sustainability is unknown. The NIA suggests against periodic Fasting as a result of uncertainties regarding its performance as well as security, particularly for the senior.

It is an eating pattern where you switch between periods of consuming and also fasting. It does not state anything concerning which foods to eat, yet rather when you ought to consume them. There are several various intermittent fasting techniques, every one of which split the day or week into consuming periods and fasting periods—lots of people currently "fast" every day while they rest. Recurring Fasting can be as simple as extending that fast a little much longer. You can do this by avoiding the morning meal, consuming your very first dish at noontime, and also your last meal at 8 pm. Then you're practically fasting for 16 hours each day, as well as restricting your eating to an 8-hour eating window. This is one of the most preferred forms of periodic Fasting, referred to as the 16/8 approach. Regardless of what you may assume, intermittent Fasting is really rather simple. Lots of people report feeling much better and having more energy throughout a quickly.

Cravings are usually not that big of a concern, although it can be trouble initially, while your body is getting used to not eating for a prolonged amount of time. No food is enabled during the fasting period, yet you can consume water, coffee, tea, and other non-caloric beverages. Some types of periodic fasting permit percentages of healthy foods throughout the fasting duration. Taking supplements is generally permitted while fasting, as long as there are no calories in them. In a globe filled with a crash diet, it is essential to start with the understanding that periodic Fasting is not a diet regimen, it's a nutrition method-- or rather, a series of various procedures. At its core, Intermittent Fasting is a pattern of eating that cycles in between periods of fasting and also consuming. And also, instead of defining which foods you can (as well as can not) eat, it instead specifies when to eat.

Just how to Do It

The 16/8 Technique. One of the most common strategies to intermittent Fasting consists of day-to-day 16-hour fasts (commonly overnight), complied with by a window of 8 hrs in which to eat. For instance, you might quick up until 11:00 am, consume a meal, have a mid-day treat, and then eat supper before 7:00 pm Important to eat the very same number of calories you normally do-- just in a smaller window of time.

Eat-Stop-Eat. This technique entails normally consuming for many days, however, doing a 24-hour rapid once or twice each week. The most popular method to do this is not eating from after supper one night up until supper time the complying with the night. It can be more difficult if you're simply starting out with Intermittent Fasting.

While it can feel like a huge modification from the standard 3-4 dishes each day, the technique has deep roots in our transformative history. Old hunter-gatherers fasted commonly, as the food wasn't constantly available, and they never knew when their following meal would certainly be. The body, therefore, developed to be able to operate without food for a relatively prolonged amount of time. That is to say: you won't deprive your body if you stop consuming for an extensive-time period.

How would certainly you such as to be able to slim down, heal your intestine, develop muscle mass, equilibrium your hormones, and take pleasure in lots of various other health and wellness advantages? As the study is now revealing, this can be accomplished by changing the window of time that you eat your foods, which is called "recurring fasting." This is not a new idea. The Greek and also Roman warriors would do this as part of their training program. They would certainly educate throughout the day, scavenge for berries occasionally, and afterward eat one huge meal at the end of the day.

They were solid, muscular, invigorated, as well as prepared for the fight. In the year 1900, Dr. Dewey, MD, composed a book titled The No Breakfast Plan as well as Fasting Cure. Unlike western medication beliefs, also because period, guide detailed his numerous case studies and also results revealing the results of both periodic, eventually not eat, as well as long-term Fasting. Dr. Dewey and also a team of fellow medical professionals in the late 1800s as well as into the very early 1900's helped create a cultural change towards the importance of individual hygiene and also caring for your body. Also pertinent today, your body will innately go into a state of Fasting when required. For instance: when you have a health problem, you have a tendency to not want to eat, and that is why alcohol consumption plenty of fluids is so vital.

Intermittent Fasting is when you eat the exact same quantity of calories that you would certainly in a regular day yet in a shorter window of time. This means you are consuming your typical 2000 calories in a 6-8 hour window, as well as throughout the other 16-18 hours you are not eating. This is where primarily you are skipping morning meals and then eating lunch as well as supper. Recurring fasting is not about binge consuming, followed by malnourishment or any other severe type of weight loss. Rather, it includes timing your dishes to enable regular durations of Fasting. Lasting fasting/caloric restriction has constantly been slammed for muscle mass loss and also nutrient exhaustion. This is why it is not recommended for weight administration and why unhealthy individuals battle to quick enough time to obtain the recovery benefits. Recurring Fasting removes this issue. It saves your lean muscle mass, keeps nutrient degrees, favorably influences hormonal agents involved in weight loss (leptin, insulin, and ghrelin) and renews brain cells.

Recurring Fasting has taken the Internet by a tornado. All sorts of discussions have been raving its practicality and effectiveness over the past few years. There is research that proves whatever from the benefits of weight management to advertising longevity, yet there are people who declare recurring Fasting is just one more diet pattern without adequate evidence and also evidence. This is a super-sized article regarding IF (recurring Fasting) borne out by my personal experience and also some research study. I am not saying that it is the best diet regimen remedy that every person needs to exercise, yet if you're presently looking for even more info about IF to decide whether you should begin applying it, this is for you. To make it clear, recurring Fasting is not a diet regimen plan. It must be thought about, like a diet regimen pattern. As opposed to what you must and should not eat-- like a lot of diet plan programs offered on the market-- recurring Fasting is about when you should and also shouldn't consume.

A lot of diet programs suggest you eat either basically of certain foods such as:

- Atkins diet plan: suggests low carb

- Ketogenic diet: suggests high fat, low carbohydrate

- Paleo diet plan suggests raw organic

foods consumed by early humans.

Yet intermittent Fasting is much like what it claims-- fasting. Periodic Fasting doesn't suggest raising detailed food intake or minimizing particular food consumption. You just require to fast throughout a particular period by decreasing your meal regularity with bigger sections per dish in the future. In my situation, I'm complying with among the recurring fasting variants to eat in an 8-hour home window and afterward fast for the other 16 hrs on a daily basis. This is hard for most people to accept because we have been educated that we require at least three meals a day, as well as the fitness industry after that recommends that we have small portions yet more constant meals.

WHOLESOME RECIPES
ALMOND MILK QUINOA

Cook time: 20 minutes

Servings: 1

Ingredients

- ½ cup quinoa
- ¾ cup almond milk, canned
- 2 bananas, sliced

- 1 teaspoon cinnamon
- 2 tablespoons peanut butter
- 1 teaspoon vanilla
- 1 nutmeg, crushed

Instructions

1. Add quinoa, cinnamon, almond milk, vanilla, and nutmeg to a pan and bring to a boil.
2. Reduce the heat to a simmer and cook for 15 minutes, covered. When cooked, fluff with a fork.
3 Transfer the quinoa to a bowl. Serve topped with bananas and peanut butter.

QUINOA AND SWEET POTATOES

Cook time: 40 minutes

Servings: 2

Ingredients

- ½ cup quinoa
- 2 sweet potatoes, sliced
- 1 red beet
- 2 tablespoons raw walnuts, chopped
- 2 tablespoons coconut oil, melted

- 1 tablespoon olive oil
- 1 teaspoon balsamic vinegar
- 1 lemon juice
- Lemon zest
- Pepper, salt, to taste

Instructions

1. Preheat the oven to 375°F.
2. Get a rimmed baking sheet and place the sweet potatoes and beets onto it. Drizzle with coconut oil and sprinkle with salt and pepper — Bake for 40 minutes.
3. Meanwhile, cook the quinoa as per the package instructions.
4. After the potatoes and beets are baked, transfer them to a bowl to cool. Slice the beets into tiny pieces.

5. Combine the prepared quinoa, beets, potatoes, and the rest of the ingredients in a large bowl, then serve.

HONEY BUCKWHEAT COCONUT PORRIDGE

Cook time: 15 minutes

Servings: 2

Ingredients

- ¼ cup buckwheat, toasted, ground
- 1 tablespoon coconut, shredded
- 2 tablespoons pecans, chopped
- ½ cup + 2 tablespoons coconut milk
- 1 tablespoon raw honey

- ¾ teaspoon vanilla
- ¾ cup of water
- 2 tablespoons currants
- 1 drizzle coconut syrup

Instructions

1. In a small pot, boil the coconut milk, honey, vanilla, and water. Stir in the ground buckwheat then reduce the heat to low.

2. Cook for 10 minutes, covered. Add extra liquid during the cooking if needed.

3. Transfer to a bowl and serve with shredded coconut, pecans, currants, and a drizzle of coconut syrup.

TEMPEH AND POTATO

Cook time: 20 minutes

Servings: 4

Ingredients

- 1 package (8 oz) tempeh, finely diced
- 4 red potatoes
- 6 leaves lacinato kale, stemmed, chopped

- 2 tablespoons olive oil
- 1 medium onion, chopped
- 1 medium green bell pepper, diced
- 1 teaspoon smoked paprika
- 1 teaspoon seasoning, salt-free
- Ground pepper, salt, to taste

Instructions

1. Microwave the potatoes until done but still firm. Finely chop them when cool.

2. Preheat oil in a skillet over medium heat. Sauté onions until translucent. Add tempeh, potatoes and bell pepper and sauté, stirring constantly, over medium-high heat until golden brown.

3. Stir in the kale and seasoning, then cook, stirring constantly until the mixture is a bit browned. Occasionally add water to prevent sticking if necessary.

4. Sprinkle with pepper and salt to taste. Serve hot.

BREAKFAST FRENCH TOAST

Cook time: 6 minutes

Servings: 1

Ingredients

- 2 slices bread, gluten-free
- 2 teaspoons cinnamon
- 2 tablespoons flaxseed, ground
- 6 oz. soy milk

- 2 teaspoons vanilla extract
- 1 scoop vegan protein powder

Instructions

1. Mix cinnamon, flaxseed, soy milk, vanilla extract, and protein powder in a deep baking dish. Deep the bread slices into the mixture to coat.

2. Preheat a non-stick frying pan over medium heat and toast the bread for 3 minutes per side. Enjoy!

DAIRY-FREE PUMPKIN PANCAKES

- 3 tablespoons chia seeds
- 3 tablespoons coconut oil, melted, slightly cooled
- 1 cup almond milk
- 2 teaspoons vanilla extract
- 1 tablespoon white vinegar
- 1 tablespoon maple syrup
- 1 teaspoon pumpkin pie spice

- ½ teaspoon kosher salt

Instructions

1. Combine almond milk and vinegar in a bowl. Let rest for 5 minutes.

2. Mix flour, baking powder, baking soda, chia seeds, pumpkin pie spice, and salt in a separate bowl.

3. Whisk eggs into the almond milk, then stir in pumpkin puree, coconut oil, vanilla, and maple syrup. Pour the wet ingredients into the dry ingredients and mix until blended. Add in more almond milk if the batter is thick. Place a non-stick frying pan over medium heat. Scoop out 1/3 of the batter and pour it into the pan. Cook for 1 minute, then flip to the other side and cook until golden brown. Do this with the remaining batter and serve.

PROTEIN BLUEBERRY BARS

Cook time: 5 minutes

Servings: 16

Ingredients

- ½ cup dried blueberries
- 1 ½ cups rolled oats
- ¾ cup whole almonds
- 1/3 cup ground flaxseed

- 1/3 cup walnuts
- ¼ cup sunflower seeds
- ½ cup pistachios
- 1/3 cup pepitas
- ¼ cup apple sauce
- 1/3 cup maple syrup
- 1 cup almond butter

Instructions

1. In a bowl, mix rolled oats, blueberries, almonds, flaxseed, walnuts, sunflower seeds, pistachios and pepitas together.

2. Stir in apple sauce and maple syrup. Mix in almond butter, then pour the batter into a baking sheet lined with parchment paper (paper should be big enough to cover and hang over the baking sheet edges). Firmly press down the batter using your palms, then spread evenly.

3. Refrigerate for 1 hour. Remove from the freezer afterward and lift the batter from pan by lifting from the paper. Place on a working surface and gently remove the paper. Cut the dough into 16 bars and serve.

CHICKPEA SCRAMBLE BREAKFAST BASIN]

Cook time: 10 minutcs

Servings: 2

Ingredients

For chickpea scramble:

- 1 can (15 oz.) chickpeas
- A drizzle olive oil

- ¼ white onion, diced
- 2 garlic cloves, minced
- ½ teaspoon turmeric
- ½ teaspoon pepper
- ½ teaspoon salt

For breakfast basin:

- 1 avocado, wedged
- Greens, combined
- Handful parsley, minced
  Handful cilantro, minced

Instructions

For chickpea scramble:

1. Scoop out the chickpeas and a little bit of its water into a bowl. Slightly mash the chickpeas using a fork, intentionally omitting some. Stir in turmeric, pepper and salt until adequately combined.
2. Sauté onions in olive oil until soft, then add garlic and cook for 1 minute. Stir in the chickpeas and sauté for 5 minutes.
3. For breakfast basin and serving: Get 2 breakfast basins. Layer the bottom of the basins with the combined greens. Top with chickpea scramble, parsley, and cilantro. Enjoy with avocado wedges.

QUINOA, OATS, HAZELNUT AND BLUEBERRY SALAD

Cook time: 35 minutes

Servings: 8

Ingredients

- 1 cup golden quinoa, dry
- 1 cup oats, cut into pieces
- 2 cups blueberries
- 2 cups hazelnuts, roughly chopped, toasted
- ½ cup dry millet
- 2 large lemons, zested, juiced
- 3 tablespoons olive oil, divided
- ½ cup maple syrup
- 1 cup Greek yogurt
- 1 (1-inch) piece fresh ginger, peeled, cut
- ¼ teaspoon nutmeg

Instructions

1. Combine quinoa, oats and millet in a large bowl. Rinse, drain and set aside.

2. Add one tablespoon olive oil into a saucepan and place over medium-high heat. Cook the rinsed grains in it for 3 minutes. Add 4 ½ cups water and salt. Add the zest of 1 lemon and ginger.

3. When the mixture boils, cover the pot and cook in reduced heat for 20 minutes. Remove from heat. Let rest for 5 minutes. Uncover and fluff with a fork. Discard the ginger and layer the grains on a large baking sheet. Let cool for 30 minutes.

4. Transfer the grains into a large bowl and mix in the remaining lemon zest.

5. Combine the juice of both lemons with the remaining olive oil in a separate bowl. Stir in the yogurt, maple syrup,

and nutmeg. Pour the mixture into the grains and stir. Mix in the blueberries and hazelnuts. Refrigerate overnight, then serve.

BUTTERED OVERNIGHT OATS

Cook time: 5 minutes

Servings: 1

Ingredients

- ¾ cup rolled oats

- ½ teaspoon cinnamon
- 2 tablespoons chia seeds
- 1 ripe banana, mashed
- 2 tablespoons peanut butter
- ½ cup + 1 tbsp. water
- 1 cup vanilla almond milk, unsweetened
- 2 tablespoons maple syrup
- 1 pinch salt

Instructions

1. Get a mason jar and add oats, cinnamon, chia seeds and salt to it. Combine properly. Stir in almond milk, mashed banana, and ½ cup water.

2. Mix peanut butter and 1 tablespoon water in a bowl then add into the jar and stir. Stir in the maple syrup and refrigerate overnight. Serve.

PROTEIN BREAKFAST BURRITO

Cook time: 30 minutes

Servings: 4

Ingredients

For tofu:

- 1 package (12 oz.) firm tofu
- ¼ cup parsley, minced
- 1 tablespoon hummus
- 1 teaspoon oil
- 1 teaspoon nutritional yeast
- ½ teaspoon cumin
- ½ teaspoon chili powder
- ¼ teaspoon salt
- 3 garlic cloves

For vegetables:

- 5 baby potatoes, sliced into pieces
- 2 cups kale, chopped

- 1 tablespoon water
- 1 medium red bell pepper, sliced thin
- ½ teaspoon ground cumin
- ½ teaspoon chili powder
- 1 pinch salt

  For assembling:

- 4 large tortillas
- 1 medium avocado, ripe, chopped
- Hot sauce
- Cilantro

Instructions

1. Preheat the oven to 400 F.
2. Squeeze out excess moisture from tofu by wrapping it in a towel and placing a heavy object on top. Crumble into fine pieces and set aside.
3. Place potatoes and red pepper onto a parchment paper lined baking sheet,

then sprinkle with water, cumin, chili powder and salt. Toss and bake for 22 minutes. In the 17 minutes' mark, add kale, toss and bake for extra 5 minutes.

4. Preheat a skillet over medium heat. Add oil, garlic and tofu once skillet is hot, then sauté for 8 minutes, stirring frequently.

5. Meanwhile, mix hummus, yeast, chili powder, cumin and salt in a bowl, then add 2 tablespoons water. Stir in parsley. Pour the mixture into the tofu and cook until slightly browned. Place aside.

6. Roll out each tortilla and scoop a large portion of potato mixture, tofu mixture, avocado, cilantro and a bit of hot sauce into the middle of each tortilla. Roll up and seal the seam, then serve immediately.

BREAKFAST HUMMUS TOAST

Cook time: 5 minutes

Servings: 1

Ingredients

- 2 slices wheat bread, sprouted, toasted
- ¼ cup hummus
- 1 tablespoon sunflower seeds, unsalted, roasted
- 1 tablespoon hemp seeds

Instructions

1. Top the toasted breads with hummus, sunflower seeds and hemp seeds. Enjoy!

ALMOND MILK BANANA SMOOTHIE

Cook time: 5 minutes

Servings: 1

Ingredients

- 2 bananas, frozen
- ¾ cup almond milk
- 2 tablespoons peanut butter
- 2 tablespoons cacao powder

  For topping:

- ½ banana, sliced
- Chocolate granola

Instructions

1. Blend bananas, almond milk, peanut butter and cacao powder in a blender until smooth.
2. Transfer to a bowl and top with sliced banana and granola. Enjoy!

NUTRITIOUS TOASTED CHICKPEAS

Cook time: 30 minutes

Servings: 2

Ingredients

- 2 cup chickpeas, cooked
- 6 bread slices, toasted
- 2 large tomatoes, skinned, chopped
- 2 tablespoons olive oil
- 3 small shallots, diced
- ½ teaspoon cinnamon
- ¼ teaspoon smoked paprika
- ½ teaspoon sweet paprika
- 2 large garlic cloves, diced
- ½ teaspoon sugar
- Black pepper, to taste
- ½ teaspoon salt

Instructions

1. Heat olive oil in a frying pan. Sauté shallots, stirring frequently until almost translucent. Add garlic then sauté until garlic is softened.

2. Add the spices into the pan. Cook for 1 minute, stirring frequently.

3. Add the tomatoes into the pan. Add some water, then cook on medium-low heat until a thick sauce forms.

4. Stir in the chickpeas and cook for 3 minutes, then sprinkle with black pepper, sugar and salt.

5. Top toasted bread with the chickpeas mixture and serve.

ALMOND MILK CHAI QUINOA

Cook time: 30 minutes

Servings: 1

Ingredients

- ½ cup quinoa, rinsed
- 1 cup almond milk
- 1 chai tea bag

Instructions

1. Combine quinoa, almond milk and chai tea bag in a pan and bring to a boil. Remove the tea bag then reduce the heat. Cook, covered, for 20 minutes.
2. Remove from fire and leave covered 10 minutes. Enjoy!

TOMATO TOFU BREAKFAST TACOS

Cook time: 20 minutes

Servings: 3

Ingredients

- 10 small corn tortillas, warmed
- 1 block (16 oz.) firm tofu, sprouted, drained, rinsed, crumbled
- 3 Roma tomatoes
- ½ tablespoon olive oil
- I lime juice
- ½ medium red onions, diced
- 1 tablespoon paprika, smoked
- 1 red bell pepper, roasted, chopped
- 1 poblano pepper, cored, diced
- 1 tablespoon chili powder
- ¾ teaspoon salt + ¼ tsp. to taste

  For toppings:

- 1 ripe avocado, peeled, mashed with lime juice + salt

Instructions

1. Heat olive oil over medium heat in a large frying pan. Sauté the red onion and poblano pepper for 5 minutes.

2. In the meantime, blend the Roma tomatoes until properly chopped, but not thoroughly blended. Set aside.

3. To the frying pan, add smoked paprika, chili powder, red pepper and salt. Sauté for 1 minute. Add the Roma tomatoes and stir. Stir in the crumbled tofu, then cook for 10 minutes, stirring infrequently. Add the lime juice and cook for 1 minute. Remove from heat and season with ¼ teaspoon salt.

4. Top each tortilla with the tofu mixture and mashed avocado then enjoy.

PEANUT BUTTER OATS

Cook time: 10 minutes

Servings: 2

Ingredients

- 1 cup rolled oats
- 2 tablespoons peanut butter
- 1 ½ cups almond milk
- 1 scoop vanilla protein powder

Instructions

1. In a bowl, stir the oats, almond milk, peanut butter, and protein powder together.
2. Cover and refrigerate for 2 hours. Serve afterward.

PROTEIN PANCAKES

Cook time: 15 minutes

Servings: 6

Ingredients

- 1 cup all-purpose flour

- ¼ cup brown rice protein powder
- 1 tablespoon baking powder
- 2 tablespoons maple syrup
- 1 cup of water
- ½ teaspoon salt

Instructions

1. In a bowl, combine all dry ingredients.
2. Mix in maple syrup and water, plus more water if necessary.
3. Preheat a non-stick frying pan over medium heat. Scoop a portion of the mixture into the pan and cook until bubbles form in the center of the pancake. Flip and cook for several more minutes. Do this with the remaining pancakes batter and enjoy!

SAVORY VEGAN OMELET

Cook time: 25 minutes

Servings: 1

Ingredients

For the Omelet:

- ¾ cup (5 oz.) firm tofu, drained, patted dry
- 1 teaspoon cornstarch
- 2 tablespoons nutritional yeast
- Olive oil
- 2 garlic cloves, minced
- ¼ teaspoon paprika
- Black pepper and salt

For the filling:

- 1 cup veggies (tomato, spinach, etc.), sliced

Instructions

1. Preheat the oven to 375 F.

2. Heat an oven-safe skillet over medium heat then add olive oil and garlic. Cook garlic for 2 minutes.

3. Add garlic and the remaining ingredients (except for the vegetables) to a food processor and mix until smooth and combined. Add 1 ½ tablespoons water. Set aside.

4. Add more olive oil to the skillet. Add the vegetables and sprinkle with pepper and salt. Cook until done, then set aside.

5. Turn off the heat. Ensure the skillet is coated with enough oil. Add ¼ of the vegetables and add the tofu mixture on top. Spread the tofu mixture across the entire skillet using a spoon but don't create gaps in it.

6. Place on the stove and cook over medium heat for 5 minutes. Bake in the oven for 15 minutes. In the 13 minutes' mark, add the remaining vegetables on top the omelet and cook for extra 2 minutes.

7. Remove from the oven. Fold over with a spatula and serve.

PROTEIN PATTIES

Cook time: 15 minutes

Servings: 5

Ingredients

- 1 can (15 oz.) chickpeas
- 1 teaspoon fennel seeds
- 1 teaspoon caraway seeds
- 1 tablespoon ground flax seeds
- 1 tablespoon tamari
- 2 tablespoons water
- 2 garlic cloves, peeled, chopped
- 1 teaspoon turmeric
- 1 teaspoon dried sage
- Pepper, salt, to taste

Instructions

1. Preheat the oven to 300 F.

2. Pulse all the ingredients in a food processor until smooth. Set aside.

3. Brush the skillet with vegetable oil and place over medium heat.

4. Spoon the mixture into the skillet. Shape into a patty using the back of the spoon, then season with salt, pepper, and paprika. Cook for 7 minutes flip over and cook for extra 7 minutes.

5. Transfer to a baking sheet and bake for 15 minutes. Serve warm.

VEGAN CHICKPEA PANCAKE

Cook time: 10 minutes

Servings: 2

Ingredients

- ½ cup chickpea flour
- ¼ teaspoon baking powder
- ½ cup + 2 tablespoons water
- 1 green onion, finely chopped
- ¼ cup red pepper, finely chopped
- 1/8 teaspoon ground black pepper
- ¼ teaspoon garlic powder
- ¼ teaspoon salt

Instructions

1. Preheat a skillet over medium heat.
2. Mix the chickpea flour, baking powder, garlic powder, pepper, and salt in a

bowl. Stir in the water. Mix for 15 seconds, then stir in onions and pepper.

3. Spray the skillet with non-stick cooking spray.

4. Pour in the batter and spread it out. Cook for 6 minutes flip carefully to the other side and cook for 5 minutes.

5. Serve with the desired toppings.

PROTEIN PUDDING

Cook time: 5 minutes

Servings: 1

Ingredients

- ¼ cup quinoa, cooked
- 2 tablespoons chia seeds
- 2 tablespoons hemp hearts
- ¾ cup cashew milk
- 2 tablespoons maple syrup
- ¼ teaspoon vanilla powder
- 1 pinch cinnamon

Instructions

1. Combine all the ingredients in a jar. Close the lid and refrigerate for 2 hours.
2. Remove from the fridge and serve.

GLUTEN-FREE TOFU QUICHE

Cook time: 90 minutes

Servings: 8

Ingredients

For the crust:

- 3 potatoes, grated
- 2 tablespoons vegan butter, melted
- ¼ teaspoon of sea salt
- ¼ teaspoon pepper

For the filling:

- 12 oz. extra-firm silken tofu, patted dry
- 1 cup broccoli, chopped
- ¾ cup cherry tomatoes halved
- 3 tablespoons hummus
- 2 tablespoons nutritional yeast
- 1 medium onion, diced
- 3 garlic cloves, chopped

- Black pepper, salt, to taste

Instructions

1. Preheat the oven to 450 F. Lightly spray a 10-inch pie pan with non-stick spray.

2. Place 3 cups of grated potatoes onto a clean towel and squeeze out the excess moisture. Transfer to the pie pan. Drizzle with melted butter and sprinkle with salt and pepper. Toss to coat. Using your fingers, gently press the content into an even layer.

3. Place into the oven and bake for 30 minutes. Take out the crust and set aside. Reduce the oven temperature to 400 F.

4. Add vegetables and garlic to the baking sheet. Sprinkle with 2 tablespoons of olive oil, pepper, and salt. Toss properly to coat. Bake for 30 minutes, then set aside. Set the oven to 375°F.

5. Mix tofu, hummus, nutritional yeast, black pepper and salt in a food processor.

6. Transfer the baked vegetables to a bowl. Add the tofu mixture and toss to coat. Add the mixture to the potato crust, then spread into an even layer.

7. Bake for 40 minutes at 375°F. Serve warm.

PUMPKIN OATMEAL

Cook time: 5 minutes

Servings: 2

Ingredients

- ½ cup rolled oats
- ¼ cup pumpkin puree
- ½ cup almond milk
- ¼ teaspoon vanilla extract
- 3 tablespoon PB2
- ¼ teaspoon instant coffee granules
- ½ cup water + more if needed
- ½ teaspoon pumpkin pie spice
- Pinch of salt

Instructions

1. Boil ½ cup milk + ½ cup water in a pan, then add oats. Cook for 2 minutes in

medium heat. Stir in the pumpkin puree and cook for several minutes more.

2. Meanwhile, gradually add water to the PB2 and mix until you get the desired consistency. Add coffee, stir well to combine, and set aside.

3. As the liquid gets dissolved, stir in vanilla extract, pumpkin pie spice and a pinch of salt.

4. Once cooked to your desire, transfer to a bowl. Top with PB2 mixture and serve.

BREAKFAST BERRY QUINOA

Cook time: 20 minutes

Servings: 4

Ingredients

- 1 cup quinoa, rinsed
- 2 cups fresh blackberries
- 1/3 cup pecans, chopped, toasted
- 4 teaspoons organic agave nectar
- 1 cup low-fat milk
- 1 cup of water½ teaspoon ground cinnamon

Instructions

1. Preheat the oven to 350 F and roast pecans for 6 minutes. Set aside for topping.
2. In a medium saucepan placed over high heat, bring water, milk, and quinoa to a

bowl. Lower the temperature to medium-low and cook for 15 minutes, covered.

3. Remove from heat and let stand for 15 minutes, covered. Mix in the blackberries and cinnamon. Share the quinoa among four plates. Serve with pecan topping and a drizzle of agave nectar.

BEAN LENTIL SALAD WITH LIME DRESSING

Cook time: 20 minute

Servings: 5

Ingredients

- 1 cup green lentils, uncooked
- 15 oz. can black beans, rinsed, drained
- 2 Roma tomatoes, finely diced
- 2/3 cup cilantro, stemmed, roughly chopped
- ½ small red onion, finely diced
- 1 red bell pepper, finely diced

  For the dressing:

- 1 lime, juiced
- 1 teaspoon Dijon mustard
- 2 garlic cloves, minced
- ½ teaspoon oregano
- 1 teaspoon cumin

- 1/8 teaspoon salt

Instructions

1. Cook lentils according to package instructions. Drain.

2. Mix all dressing ingredients in a small bowl and set aside.

3. Add the black beans, lentils, tomatoes, bell pepper and onions into a bowl. Sprinkle the dressing on top and toss to coat. Add the cilantro and toss lightly. Enjoy!

LENTIL ARUGULA SALAD

Cook time: 7 minutes

Servings: 2

Ingredients

- 1 cup (15 oz) brown lentils, cooked
- 1 handful arugula, washed
- ¾ cup (100g) cashews
- 6 sun-dried tomatoes in oil, chopped
- 3 whole-wheat bread sliced, cut big pieces
- 2 tablespoons balsamic vinegar
- 3 tablespoons olive oil
- 1 onion
- 1 jalapeno pepper, chopped
- Pepper and salt, to taste

Instructions

1. Place a frying pan over low heat and roast the cashews for 3 minutes. Transfer to a salad bowl.

2. Sauté onions in 1/3 olive oil for 3 minutes on low heat. Add jalapeno and dried tomatoes and cook for about 2 minutes. Transfer to a bowl.

3. Add the remaining olive oil to the pan and fry the bread until crunchy. Sprinkle with pepper and salt. Set aside.

4. Add arugula to the bowl containing sautéed tomato mixture. Add lentils and toss to combine — season with pepper, salt and balsamic vinegar.

5. Serve with the crunchy bread.

RED CABBAGE AND CUCUMBER SALAD WITH SEITAN

Cook time: 10 minutes

Servings: 1-2

Ingredients

For the salad:

- ½ small head red cabbage, shredded
- 1 package (8 oz.) seitan, cut into strips
- 1 small cucumber, sliced
- 3 green onions, thinly sliced
- 1 tablespoon olive oil
- 3 garlic cloves, minced
- ¾ teaspoon mild curry powder

For the dressing:

- 1/3 cup mango chutney
- 1/3 cup peanut butter

Instructions

1. Heat 2 teaspoons olive oil over medium heat in a pan. Sauté seitan for 7 minutes. Add remaining olive oil and garlic, then cook for 30 seconds. Season with curry powder and cook for extra 2 minutes. Turn off the heat and keep warm.

2. In a blender, combine peanut butter, chutney, and 1/3 cup water, process until smooth.

3. Place cabbage and cucumber into a bowl. Drizzle with the peanut butter mixture and toss properly. Top with seitan and green onions and serve.

PROTEIN PACKED CHICKPEAS AND KIDNEY BEANS SALAD

Cook time: 5 minute

Servings: 2

Ingredients

- 1 can chickpeas, drained, rinsed
- 1 can red kidney beans, drained, rinsed
- ½ cup feta cheese, crumbled
- 1 cup parsley, chopped
- Olive oil
- 1 lemon juice
- 3 scallions, chopped
- 1 small ginger, grated
- 1 medium onion, diced
- 2 garlic cloves, minced
- 1 pinch red chili flakes
- Black pepper and salt

Instructions

1. Sauté onions in 1 tablespoon olive oil until golden. Add ginger, garlic, and chili and sauté till garlic is fragrant. Set aside to cool.

2. In a salad bowl, combine chickpeas, kidney beans, feta cheese, scallions, parsley, lemon juice, pepper, salt, cooled garlic mixture, and some olive oil. Toss well to combine correctly and enjoy!

QUICK CHICKPEAS AND SPINACH SALAD

Cook time: 7 minutes

Servings: 2

Ingredients

- 1 can chickpeas, drained, rinsed
- 1 handful spinach
- 1 small handful raisins
- 3.5 oz. feta cheese, chopped
- 4 tablespoons olive oil
- 3 teaspoons honey
- ½ tablespoon lemon juice
- ½ teaspoon chili flakes
- ½ teaspoon cumin
- 1 pinch salt

Instructions

1. Add chickpeas, cheese, and spinach to a salad bowl.

2. In a separate bowl, mix honey, lemon juice, olive oil, and raisins. Stir in chili flakes, cumin, and salt. Drizzle over the salad and serve.

CARROT SLAW AND TEMPEH TRIANGLES

Cook time: 5 minutes

ervings: 4

Ingredients

- 8 oz tempeh, sliced into triangles
- 4 cups carrots, shredded
- ½ cup parsley, finely chopped
- 1 tablespoon raw walnuts, crushed
- 3 tablespoons grade B maple syrup
- 1 teaspoon olive oil
- ¼ cup lemon juice
- 2 teaspoons soy sauce
- 1 small onion, diced
- 2 tablespoons tahini
- 1/8 teaspoon black pepper
- 1 tablespoon curry powder
  Pepper and salt, to taste

Instructions

1. Heat olive oil in a skillet over high heat. Once hot, add tempeh, 1 ½ tbsp. Maple syrup and soy sauce. Cook for 5 minutes, flipping occasionally until the liquid is absorbed. Remove from heat and sprinkle with crushed walnut and pepper. Set aside and keep warm.

2. Toss carrots, tahini, lemon juice, remaining maple syrup, parsley, onions and spices in a mixing bowl for some minutes. Season with pepper and salt to taste.

3. Transfer to a serving bowl. Top with tempeh triangles and serve.

CHILI TOFU

Cook time: 50 minutes

Servings: 8

Ingredients

- 1 package (14 oz.) firm tofu
- 1 can (28 oz.) kidney beans, drained
- 1 cup mushrooms, sliced
- 1 can (28 oz.) tomatoes with liquid, diced
- 1 can (14 oz.) tomato sauce
- 3 tablespoons vegetable oil
- 1 green bell pepper, diced
- 1 onion, diced
- ¼ teaspoon cayenne pepper
- 3 tablespoons chili powder
- ½ teaspoon cumin
- 3 garlic cloves, minced
- Pepper and salt, to taste

Instructions

1. Sauté tofu in vegetable oil over medium-high heat for 3 minutes.

2. Add in the onions, green pepper, mushrooms, garlic, cayenne, cumin, chili powder, pepper, and salt and cook for 5 minutes.

3. Stir in tomato sauce, kidney beans, diced tomatoes with the liquid, and bring everything to a simmer. Cover and cook for an extra 45 minutes. Serve.

LENTIL SOUP (VEGAN)

Cook time: 50 minutes

Servings: 4

Ingredients

- 1 cup dry brown lentils
- 1 carrot, sliced
- 2 bay leaves
- 1 teaspoon vegetable oil
- 4 cups vegetable broth
- 1 onion, sliced
- ¼ teaspoon thyme, dried
- Pepper and salt, to taste

Instructions

1. Sauté onions and carrots in vegetable oil for 5 minutes. Mix in vegetable broth, lentils, bay leaves, pepper, and salt, stir well to combine.

2. Lower the heat to a simmer. Cook for 45 minutes, covered. Discard the bay leaves and serve.

HOT BLACK BEANS AND POTATO

Cook time: 25 minute

Servings: 5

Ingredients

- 1 can (15 oz.) black beans
- 2 small sweet potatoes, peeled, chopped
- 2 medium carrots, sliced
- 1 can (15 oz.) tomato sauce
- 2 tablespoons olive oil
- ½ cup of water
- 1 small onion, diced
- 2 garlic cloves, minced
- 1/2 teaspoon cayenne
- ½ teaspoon garlic powder
- 1 tablespoon chili powder
- 1 teaspoon cumin
- ¼ teaspoon black pepper
- ½ teaspoon salt

Instructions

1. Cook garlic and onions in olive oil for 2 minutes. Add potatoes and carrots and cook for 6 minutes.

2. Lower the heat to medium-low and stir in the remaining ingredients. Cook for about 25 minutes, partially covered and stirring infrequently. Once done, serve.

LOW-FAT BEAN SOUP

Cook time: 10 minutes

Servings: 4

Ingredients

- 2 cans (15 oz each) black beans, undrained
- ½ cup of salsa
- 16 oz. vegetable broth
- 1 tablespoon chili powder

Instructions

1. Pulse 1 can beans in a food processor until almost smooth.
2. Pour the mixture into a saucepan. Add the remaining can beans, vegetable broth, salsa, and chili powder into the pan.

2. Bring to a boil, and remove from the heat. Serve and enjoy!

PROTEIN RICH VEGETABLE MINESTRONE

Cook time: 30 minutes

Servings: 6

Ingredients

- ¼ cup white quinoa, uncooked
- 1 can (28 oz.) tomatoes, diced
- 1 cup carrots, sliced
- 1 ½ cups asparagus, chopped
- 1 cup packed kale, chopped
- ½ cup frozen peas
- 1 cup zucchini, chopped
- 2 bay leaves
- 1 tablespoon olive oil
- 4 cups of water
- 1 small white onion, diced
- 3 garlic cloves, minced
- 2 teaspoons Italian seasoning

- Pepper and salt, to taste

Instructions

1. Sauté onions, garlic and carrots in olive oil over medium-high heat for 3 minutes. Stir in water, tomatoes, quinoa, bay leaves, spices, pepper and salt and bring to a boil. Cover and simmer for 20 minutes.

2. Add the remaining vegetable and cook for 10 minutes. Taste and adjust seasonings if needed and serve hot.

QUINOA PUMPKIN SOUP

Cook time: 25 minutes

Servings: 4

Ingredients

- ½ cup quinoa
- 20 oz. can black beans, rinsed, drained
- 3 cups pumpkin, cubed
- 2 bay leaves
- 5 cups vegetable broth
- 1 tablespoon olive oil
- 1 onion, diced
- 5 garlic cloves, diced
- 1 red chili pepper, diced
- ½ teaspoon dried oregano
- 1 teaspoon ground cumin
- ½ teaspoon red pepper flakes, crushed

Instructions

1. Sauté onions in olive oil over medium until translucent. Stir in red chili pepper and garlic and sauté until aromatic. Mix in the pumpkin and spices and cook for a few minutes.

2. Pour in quinoa and 2 cups vegetable broth, then bring to a boil. Cook for extra 5 minutes, then add the remaining vegetable broth and cook until boiled. Stir in beans and bay leaves. Lower the heat and simmer for 10 minutes. Serve with avocados.

RED LENTIL SOUP WITH FARRO

Cook time: 32 minutes

Servings: 4

Ingredients

- ½ cup red lentils
- ½ cup quick-cook farro
- 1 cup kale, stemmed, chopped
- 1 cup carrots, grated
- 2 tablespoons olive oil
- 5 cups vegetable broth
- 1 small onion, grated
- 1 small zucchini, grated
- 1 ½ teaspoon turmeric
- ½ teaspoon cumin
- ¼ teaspoon pepper
- 1 ½ teaspoons salt

  For breadcrumbs:

- Eight slices French baguette, cubed

- Olive oil
- One garlic clove, minced
- Salt, to taste

Instructions

1. Sauté onion, carrots, and zucchini in olive oil over medium heat for 2 minutes. Stir in turmeric, cumin, pepper, and salt, then cook for 3 minutes.

2. Add the chicken broth and bring everything to a boil. Add lentils and farro and cook for about 20 minutes over low heat.

3. In the meantime, pulse bread and garlic in a food processor until done. Transfer to a baking sheet and sprinkle with olive oil and salt — Bake for 7 minutes.

4. Once the lentil soup has cooked for 15 minutes, add kale and cook for 5

minutes. Serve topped with the breadcrumbs.

MOROCCAN PUMPKIN SOUP

Cook time: 50 minutes

Servings: 4-6

Ingredients

- 3 lbs pumpkin, peeled, seeded, chopped
- 2 carrots, roughly chopped
- 1/3 cup split peas
- 3 tablespoons olive oil
- 3 tablespoons white miso paste
- 1 onion, diced
- 1 cinnamon stick
- 1 chili, finely chopped
- 1 garlic, finely chopped
- 1 small ginger, thinly sliced
- 1 ½ teaspoons cumin seeds

Instructions

1. Cook garlic, onions and salt in olive oil over low heat for 3 minutes. Add all the spices and sauté until fragrant.

2. Stir in pumpkin, carrots, and peas. Pour in 6 cups of water and bring to a boil. Simmer for extra 30 minutes. Remove and discard the cinnamon stick.

3. Using an immersion blender, puree the soup until smooth, then let cool. Stir in the miso paste and serve just after that.

MEXICAN CHICKPEA AND TOMATILLOS POZOLE

Cook time: 20 minutes

Servings: 2-4

Ingredients

- 1 ½ cups chickpeas, cooked
- 10 tomatillos, peeled, washed
- 2 cups of water
- 1 cup cilantro, chopped
- 4 garlic cloves
- ¼ onion, sliced
- 1 whole serrano chile
- 1 teaspoon salt, or to taste

Instructions

1. Add tomatillos, cilantro, onion, garlic, and water into a large pot. Cook, covered until tomatillos are very soft.

2. Add salt to taste, and puree using an immersion blender, blend the vegetables until properly combined. Stir in the chickpeas and serrano chile.

3. Reduce the heat to low and add more water if needed. Enjoy with your desired toppings.

VEGAN FRENCH ONION SOUP

Cook time: 115 minutes

Servings: 2-4

Ingredients

For caramelized onions:

- 4 white onions
- ¼ cup olive oil

  For the soup:

- 4 yellow onions
- 1 ½ cups French green lentils
- 1 cup fennel stalks, cut into thin slices
- 1 tablespoon tarragon leaves
- 1 bay leaf
- 3 vegetable bouillon cube, salt-free
- 2 tablespoons + ¼ cup olive oil
- 8 cups of water
- 6 tablespoons dry white wine

- 1 tablespoon Sherry vinegar
- 1 tablespoon fresh lemon juice
- ½ teaspoon black pepper
- 1 tablespoon + 1 teaspoon salt
- 2 tablespoons fresh thyme
- 2 garlic cloves, minced

Instructions

For the onions:

1. Slice onions into thin half circles. Cook on medium heat, infrequently stirring, for 20 minutes (without oil).
2. Pour in ¼ cup olive oil. Scrape the bottom of the pan using a wooden spatula. Stir and reduce the heat to medium-low. Cook for 20 minutes, stirring infrequently. Set aside.

For the soup:

1. In a separate pan, add one tablespoon wine. Deglaze the pan by scraping the bottom of the pan with a wooden spatula. Let rest for 10 minutes.

2. Pour in 2 more tablespoons wine, deglaze and cook for 10 minutes. Add an extra tablespoon wine, deglaze and turn the heat offseason with salt.

3. Combine lentils, water, bay leaf, and two sprigs thyme in a large pot. Cook until it boils. Simmer on medium-low heat for extra 20 minutes. Remove and discard the bay leaf and thyme sprigs.

4. Meanwhile, sauté sliced fennel stalks and garlic in olive oil over medium-low heat until garlic is fragrant.

5. Add tarragon, bouillon cubes, and two tablespoons thyme. Mash the bouillon. Stir the ingredients, then add one

tablespoon wine. Cook the stalks, frequently stirring until they turn golden. Pour in the remaining wine. Scrape the bottom of the pan with a spatula, then cook for some minutes more.

6. Pour the sautéed fennel stalk mixture and the caramelized onions into the cooked lentils. Mix in 2 tablespoons water, sherry vinegar, lemon juice, pepper, and salt, then cook for some minutes before serving.

TOFU BACON BEAN SALAD

Cook time: 15 minutes

Servings: 4

Ingredients

- 12 slices Tofu Bacon, cut into pieces
- 1 can black beans, drained
- 1 large head romaine lettuce, washed, chopped
- 1 avocado, sliced
- 1 can organic corn
- 24 cherry tomatoes
- ½ cup cilantro, chopped
- Fresh lime juice, for dressing

Instructions

1. Divide all the ingredients between 4 plates and drizzle with lime juice dressing.

2. Toss well to combined. Enjoy immediately.

RICE NOODLES SALAD FOR THE SUMMER

Cook time: 5 minutes

Servings: 2

Ingredients

- 1 can (8 oz.) rice noodles
- 1 cup carrots, shredded
- 1/3 cup peanuts
- 2 scallions, chopped
- ½ teaspoon black sesame seeds
- ½ red bell pepper, thinly sliced

  For the dressing:

- 1/3 cup peanut butter
- 3 tablespoons sriracha
- 1 tablespoon rice vinegar
- 2 tablespoons hot water
- 2 garlic cloves, minced

Instructions

1. Prepare noodles according to package instructions. Drain and rinse with cold water to cool. Set aside.
2. Mix all the dressing ingredients in a bowl and set aside.
3. Toss the noodles with the rest of the ingredients. Mix with the peanut butter dressing and serve.

PROTEIN POWER SALAD

Cook time: 25 minutes

Servings: 4

Ingredients

For the salad:

- ¾ cup red quinoa, rinsed, uncooked
- 1 cup cherry tomatoes, halved
- 4 cups mild green
- 1 cup hothouse cucumber, chopped
- ½ cup kalamata olives halved
- 1/3 cup toasted Marcona almonds
- 1/3 cup prepared Lemon Oregano Vinaigrette

For the dressing:

- 2 tablespoons lemon juice
- 2 tablespoons white wine vinegar
- 1/3 cup extra virgin olive oil

- 1 tablespoon + 1 teaspoon maple syrup
- 1 tablespoon oregano leaves
- 1½ teaspoons Dijon mustard
- 1 garlic clove
- ⅛ teaspoon black pepper
- ⅛ teaspoon salt

Instructions

1. Bring quinoa and 1 ½ cups water to a boil in a pan. Reduce the heat to a simmer and cook for 15 minutes, covered. Remove from heat and let rest for 5 minutes, still covered. Afterward, rinse in a fine-mesh sieve under cold water and set aside.

2. Using a blender, blend all the dressing ingredients, except olive oil. Lastly, slowly pour in olive oil while the

mixer is still on. Set aside for dressing.

3. To make the salad: Combine all the salad ingredients (including the cooked quinoa). Pour the dressing over the salad and toss. Enjoy!

MUSHROOMS LEMON SALAD

Cook time: 40 minutes

Servings: 2

Ingredients

- 4 cups Swiss brown and button mushrooms, sliced
- ½ cup French green lentils
- 2 tablespoons parsley, roughly chopped
- ½ cup arugula
- 1 ½ tablespoon lemon juice
- 5 tablespoons extra virgin olive oil
- 2 cups of water
- ½ shallot, chopped
- 2 garlic cloves, minced
- ¼ teaspoon chili flakes
- Pepper and salt, to taste

Instructions

1. Bring lentils and 2 cups water to a boil in a pan. Simmer for 25 minutes. Drain and set aside.

2. Cook mushrooms part by part in a frying pan (without oil), over medium heat for 3 minutes, flipping over half-way through. Set aside.

3. Sauté shallots in 2 teaspoons olive oil over medium-low heat until slightly golden. Add in the mushrooms, chili flakes, and garlic and cook for 2 minutes. Set aside.

4. Drizzle the salad with the remaining olive oil and lemon juice. Sprinkle with pepper and salt to taste. Top with parsley and arugula, then serve!

ALL-IN-ONE ROASTED SQUASH AND FREEKEH LUNCH SALAD

Cook time: 20 minutes

Servings: 4

Ingredients

For the squash:

- 1 butternut squash, peeled, diced
- 1 tablespoon maple syrup
- 2 tablespoons olive oil
- ½ teaspoon black pepper
- 1 teaspoon kosher salt

For the freekeh and kale:

- 1 cup freekeh, uncooked
- 8 cups kale, chopped
- 1 tablespoon olive oil
- 2 ½ cups water
- ¼ teaspoon ground nutmeg

- ¼ teaspoon red pepper flakes, crushed
- 2 teaspoons garlic, minced
- ¼ teaspoon black pepper
- 1 ½ teaspoon kosher salt

For the dressing:

- 1 tablespoon maple syrup
- 2 tablespoon apple cider vinegar
- 1 tablespoon orange juice
- ½ cup olive oil
- ½ cup dried cranberries
- ½ cup toasted walnuts, chopped, halved
- 2 teaspoons Dijon mustard
- ¼ teaspoon black pepper
- 1 teaspoon kosher salt

Instructions

1. For the squash: Preheat the oven to 400°F. Place the squash on a baking sheet and sprinkle with 1 tbsp. Maple

syrup, 2 tablespoons olive oil, pepper and salt to taste. Toss properly and bake for 20 minutes, turning halfway through.

2. For the freekeh: Boil 2 ¼ cups water in a pan, sprinkle with ½ teaspoon salt. Lower the heat to medium-low and cook freekeh, covered, for 20 minutes. Turn off the heat and leave covered for 5 minutes, then fluff and set aside.

3. For the kale: Sauté kale in 1 tablespoon olive oil over medium heat for 5 minutes, stirring frequently. Add garlic, nutmeg, red pepper flakes, pepper, and salt. Stir and cook for 1 minute.

4. For the dressing: Combine maple syrup, vinegar, orange juice, mustard, pepper, and salt in a bowl. Gently pour in olive oil while mixing until well incorporated.

5. To make the salad: In the kale skillet, stir in the butternut squash, freekeh, cranberries, and walnuts. Drizzle some of the dressing on top and toss softly to coat. Transfer to serving plates, drizzle with the remaining dressing, and serve.

VEGAN CAULIFLOWER SOUP

Cook time: 25 minutes

Servings: 6

Ingredients

- 1 head (3-pound) cauliflower, cut into florets
- 2 cups split peas, cooked
- 2 tablespoons dietary yeast

- 2 tablespoons olive oil
- 7 cups of water
- 1 ½ yellow onions, chopped
- 1 ½ teaspoon ground turmeric
- Black pepper, to taste
- 1 ½ teaspoon salt

Instructions

1. Heat oil over medium heat in a saucepan, then add onions, turmeric, and salt and cook for about 10 minutes, stirring infrequently.

2. Add 2 cups of water and bring the mixture to a boil. Add cauliflower, cover, and cook for 15 minutes. Add yeast and remaining water then let it boil uncovered for about 5 minutes.

3. Blend the soup with a blender until smooth. Add more water and salt if

necessary, then add the black pepper and serve with split peas.

PANZANELLA

Cook time: 20 minutes

Servings: 4

Ingredients

- 2 slices multi-grain bread, cut into 1-inch cubes
- 12 oz. extra-firm tofu, sliced into 4 pieces
- ½ cup sun-dried tomatoes

- 1 ½ cups sprouts
- 1/3 cups peanut butter
- 2 tablespoons olive oil
- 2 tablespoons apple cider vinegar
- ½ teaspoon toasted sesame oil
- 2/3 cup hot water
- 1 garlic clove
- ¼ teaspoon red pepper flakes
- Pinch of salt

Instructions

1. Heat the oven to 375 F. Drizzle bread with olive oil and season with salt and bake for about 11 minutes Brush tofu with some olive oil, place on a baking pan and bake for about 7 minutes on each side. Cut into ½-inch slices and place into a bowl. Mix peanut butter, vinegar, sesame oil, garlic, pepper flakes and ¼ teaspoon salt in a bowl. Add hot

water to make thin the mixture. Add more pepper or salt to taste if needed. Drizzle tofu generously with the mixture and toss well to combine. Add the bread and toss slightly. Spread onto a serving dish and leave to cool slightly. Top with tomatoes and sprouts, and then serve.

NUTRITIOUS BEET HUMMUS

Cook time: 10 minutes

Servings: 8

Ingredients

- 1 can (14 oz.) chickpeas, drained, rinsed
- 1 raw golden beet, peeled, quartered
- 2 tablespoons tahini
- Sesame seeds
- 6 tablespoons fresh lemon juice

- 4 garlic cloves
- ¼ teaspoon salt
- ½ cup of ice water

Instructions

1. Peel the chickpeas then puree in a blender. Add the beets and puree well until smooth. Add lemon juice, tahini, garlic, salt, and ice water and blend for 3 minutes. Add more salt and lemon juice if necessary

2. Transfer to a serving plate, top with sesame seed and serve

WHITE BEAN SOUP WITH GREEN HERB DUMPLINGS

Cook time: 25 minutes

Servings: 6

Ingredients

White Bean Soup:

- 1 can (14 oz.) cannellini beans, drained, rinsed
- ½ cup whole wheat pastry flour
- 2 carrots, peeled and diced
- 3 tablespoons olive oil
- 5 cups of water
- 1 big onion, finely chopped
- 1 teaspoon salt

Green Herb Dumplings:

- 1 cup herbs (scallions, dill, basil), chopped
- 2 tablespoons pesto
- 1 ½ cups whole wheat pastry flour
- 2 teaspoons baking powder
- 1 ¼ cup milk
- ½ teaspoon salt

Instructions

1. Heat olive oil in a pot over medium-high heat, then fry onions and carrots in it for about 7 minutes. Stir in flour and cook for 3 minutes. Add water and salt and boil for 6 minutes. Stir in beans and boil while you prepare the herbs.

2. Mix milk and pesto properly in a bowl then add herbs.

3. In a separate bowl, combine flour, baking powder, and salt. Add the milk mixture, then mix properly to combine. Add a large tablespoon of this mixture into the boiling soup.

4. Cover and cook for 7 minutes. Flip each dumpling then cook for extra 7 minutes. Top with more herbs and serve hot.

CPSIA information can be obtained
at www.ICGtesting.com
Printed in the USA
BVHW091409030521
606339BV00005B/733

9 781802 232431